D1226365

Blue Whales

by Grace Hansen

Abdo
SUPER SPECIES
Kids

abdopublishing.com

Published by Abdo Kids, a division of ABDO, PO Box 398166, Minneapolis, Minnesota 55439.

Copyright © 2017 by Abdo Consulting Group, Inc. International copyrights reserved in all countries. No part of this book may be reproduced in any form without written permission from the publisher.

Printed in the United States of America, North Mankato, Minnesota.

052016
092016

THIS BOOK CONTAINS RECYCLED MATERIALS

Photo Credits: AP Images, iStock, Minden Pictures, Science Source, Seapics.com, Shutterstock
Paul Goldstein/Exodus/REX Shutterstock p.11

Production Contributors: Teddy Borth, Jennie Forsberg, Grace Hansen

Design Contributors: Laura Mitchell, Dorothy Toth

Cataloging-in-Publication Data

Names: Hansen, Grace, author.

Title: Blue whales / by Grace Hansen.

Description: Minneapolis, MN : Abdo Kids, [2017] | Series: Super species |
    Includes bibliographical references and index.

Identifiers: LCCN 2015959209 | ISBN 9781680805420 (lib. bdg.) |
    ISBN 9781680805987 (ebook) | ISBN 9781680806540 (Read-to-me ebook)

Subjects: LCSH: Blue whale--Juvenile literature.

Classification: DDC 599.5--dc23

LC record available at http://lccn.loc.gov/2015959209

Table of Contents

World's Biggest Animal

Blue whales are the largest whale species. They are also the biggest animals on Earth.

Blue whales can grow up to 100 feet (30 m) long. That is longer than two school buses!

100 ft

45 ft

45 ft

A blue whale can weigh

up to 200 tons (181,000 kg).

That is heavier than

33 African elephants!

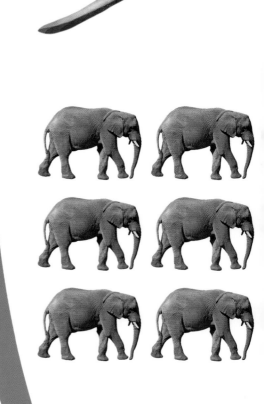

9

Body

Blue whales have wide,
flat heads. Their bodies
are very long. Their flukes
are large and triangular.

10

fluke

Blue whales do not have teeth.
They have **baleen** instead.
Baleen is like hair. But it is very
thick and tough. These hairs
are used to filter food.

Food

Blue whales eat tiny animals called **krill**. Krill float together in big groups. This makes eating them easy!

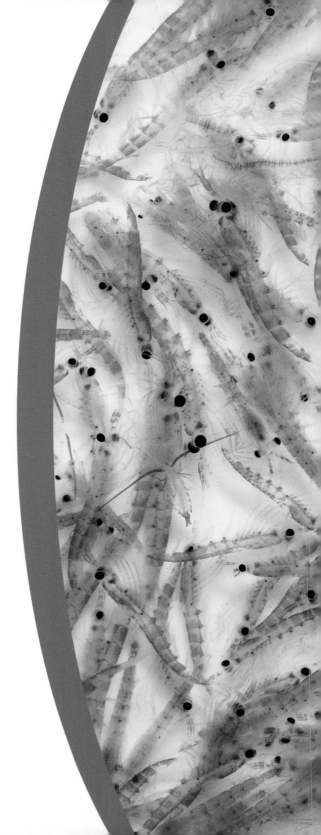

15

Blue whales scoop water and krill into their mouths. Then they push out the water through the baleen. Now, only krill are left inside their mouths. They eat about 4 tons (3,700 kg) of krill each day.

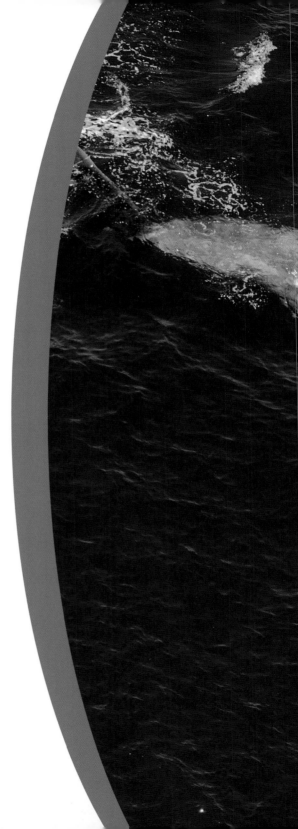

Big Babies

Baby blue whales are called calves. Calves already weigh 3 tons (2,700 kg) at birth. And they are 25 feet (7.5 m) long!

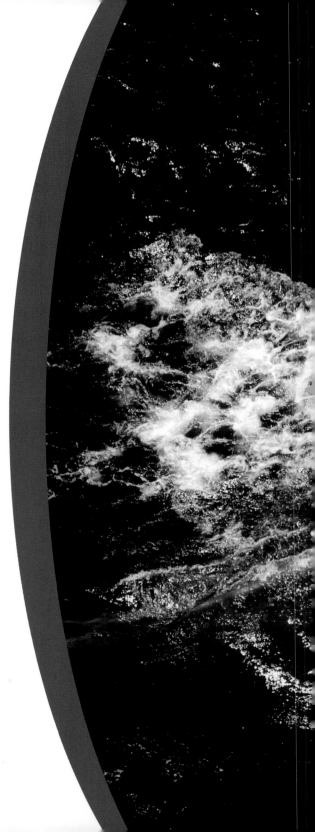

Calves drink their mothers' milk all day. They gain 200 pounds (91 kg) a day for a year! Soon, they will be as big as their parents.

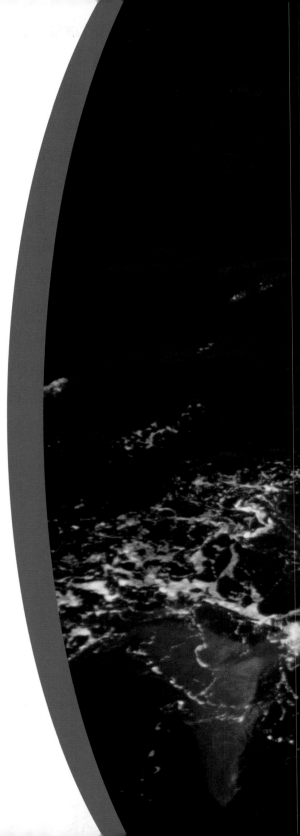

21

More Facts

- Blue whales sometimes swim with small groups.
  But they are usually alone or in pairs.

- Blue whales swim the ocean at 5 miles per hour (8 km/h).
  They can get up to 20 miles per hour (32 km/h) if needed.

- Blue whales are one of the loudest animals on Earth.
  They talk to each other through grunts, moans, and clicks.

Glossary

baleen – a tough material that hangs down from the upper jaw of a whale without teeth and is used by the whale to filter small ocean animals out of water.

fluke – one of the two halves of a whale's tail.

krill – very small creatures in the ocean that are the main food of some whales.

species – a particular group of animals that are similar and can make young animals.

Index

abdokids.com

Use this code to log on to abdokids.com and access crafts, games, videos, and more!

Abdo Kids Code:
SBK5420

24